D1605593

CONSTANTS
OF THE
MOTION

ROALD HOFFMANN

DOS MADRES

2020

DOS MADRES PRESS INC.
P.O. Box 294, Loveland, Ohio 45140
www.dosmadres.com   editor@dosmadres.com

Dos Madres is dedicated to the belief that the small press is essential to the vitality of contemporary literature as a carrier of the new voice, as well as the older, sometimes forgotten voices of the past. And in an ever more virtual world, to the creation of fine books pleasing to the eye and hand.

Dos Madres is named in honor of Vera Murphy and Libbie Hughes, the "Dos Madres" whose contributions have made this press possible.

Dos Madres Press, Inc. is an Ohio Not For Profit Corporation and a 501 (c) (3) qualified public charity. Contributions are tax deductible.

Executive Editor: Robert J. Murphy

Illustration & Book Design: Elizabeth H. Murphy
www.illusionstudios.net
Cover: Sculpture by Evert Lindfors
(photograph by Cécile Lindfors)

Typeset in Adobe Garamond Pro, Charlemagne & Copperplate
ISBN 978-1-953252-06-7
Library of Congress Control Number: 2020945569

First Edition

ACKNOWLEDGMENTS

Some of these poems were written in an old farmhouse in the plain between Lacoste and Bonnieux, in the Luberon in France, some at the Djerassi Resident Artists Program in the Santa Cruz mountains in California; I am grateful to Crystal Woodward for introducing me to Provence, and to DRAP for the opportunity to write in their inspiring surroundings. The impression that Evert Lindfors, a Swedish sculptor who worked in France (ateliers-lindfors.com), made on me is apparent in several poems. I am grateful to Cécile Lindfors for permission to reproduce an image of one of his works on the cover of this book.

Several poems in this collection have been published in periodicals, on the web, and in anthologies. I am grateful to the editors of the following for their confidence in my writing: *The Quad* (Lessons in Being Alone); *Hampden-Sydney Review (*Black on Black), *New Letters (* Singing in the Rain, Provence; Constants of the Motion), *The Sigurd Journal* (Code, Memory), *The Yale Review* (Just When We Are Safest); *Media Fields Journal* (Sustainable Development). *Beloit Poetry Journal* (With, or Against), *Southwest Review* (The Exchange), *Alabama Poetry Review* (Basket Philosophy, Tectonics).

Some of the poems in this collection have also been incorporated into a play, "Something That Belongs to You," about my mother's and my survival in the Holocaust. This play has also been published by Dos Madres Press.

DEDICATED TO CARL DJERASSI,
AND THE
DJERASSI RESIDENT ARTISTS PROGRAM
HE CREATED

TABLE OF CONTENTS

CONSTANTS
OF THE
MOTION

CONSTANTS OF THE MOTION

In mechanics, a constant of motion is a quantity that is conserved throughout the motion, imposing in effect a constraint on the motion... Common examples include energy, linear momentum, angular momentum and the Laplace-Runge-Lenz vector (for inverse-square force laws).

—*Wikipedia*

Classical:
You've swung
so far as
to risk that
top trill of
your motion.
There, poised,
where beyond
would kill, you're
all potential.
To move. Again,
and when you
do, down, it's
all kinetic, and
what drew you
there compels
you rush on.
Don't stop, please.

Equations:
No outer force,
the push/pull

of a father's
dream, career
jig. It's natural.
a caress given
a hug returned.
Neither reward,
nor dissipation
figure much
in the meet
equations
of our motion.

Quantum:
So the world
plays tough –
torn menisci,
nixed grant.
And then you
saunter by
with simple gifts –
a touch, sweet
love. I am. But
now the test.
Imagine
it turned around:
We fall in love,
settings "high,"
and then – in

just a trice
things fall apart,
shoes land, the
world turns on
its random wear
and tear. Where
are we, dear?

Time rate change:
Together, still
But the equations,
heartless, say
stasis is not
an option. Move.
Just move on,
kids, up, out;
mothers die, oh
wilting, stents.
To the parts
that cry and
muse, love's left,
the sole constant
of the motion.

I
PROVENCE

THE CULTIVATED LAND

1

A brown and reddish land,
walked in midwinter terrace
by cherry terrace, cherries
where once were apricots,
here in straight, yet un-
dulating rows, guidewires
easing machine picking,
past stone walls, stacked
firewood, past the rusty
tangle of uprooted vines,
to the smoke of my cabin.

2

The sculptor sees a dead bird
and from its contours a clay
one lifts inward on a crooked
single wing. He sketches
a woman's arthritic bend
in a field, bakes chimeras,
the hybrid animal/human
scream and jump. Don't
begin abstract, says Evert,
making what can never be.

3

The hand of animal man,
hungry and reproducing,
passes over this land and
the land, contoured, says
you have made me, and
I you...the toolmaker, per-
force natural. But in me
enzymes churn, half
their sulfur atoms out
of an acid plant; where
oh where is common
ground? I've walked that
factory, seen its plans, I've
felt the workers' hands.

4

Or shall we say it is all
manmade? Bred as the vine,
grafted on American roots,
all that earth delineated,
waters channeled, the hare
shot in the morning, ground
soaked with herbicide. But
what of the wind wild and
the November snow storm?
The oak leaves, the jagged
gall growth, the rosehip's
resistant turn red to black?

5

It would have made sense
to take the problem to the ap-
paratus, to watch a needle
swing, and say: this is ...
68.4% natural, the rest...
And Evert's clay bird?

6

This is the cultivated land,
the meeting ground of cherries
and the memory of apricots
that were, of wires and un-
supported vines, of the wine-
makers steel tanks, trained
dogs under oak trees stunted
for truffles, the unromantic
ground where lavender is
a century old; where people
were kind, bred animals and
killed each other for a creed,
where every stone terrace
says I intervene. Your mud
is on my boots, oh dear land.

7

I listen to the land as I walk;
its distant dogs baying for me
in cross cadences, the whine
of a saw, a truck on a hill,
crows talking crow talk. Back
home, a horsefly is hell-bent
on the way in; I hear the logs
spitting as the fire cools. Later,
the evening wind in my ears,
the mistral in the ears of the house.

8

The branches of the one cherry
to be pruned cradle a plastic water
bottle, half full. It's waiting,
for the pruner, for tomorrow.

SINGING IN THE RAIN, PROVENCE

for Evert Lindfors

Walking in rain
in a yellow slicker

is as close as I'll get
to dancing; no one

is out to watch me,
either, though I

did pass some sad
dogs, and two English-

women. My umbrella
is furled, back pain,

but with good boots,
a hood, who knows

what I might see
down this old path,

maybe wild boars
mating with pigs.

Or the rain could
twist, like an in-

tegral sign, or
its drops reach and

seize hold, in lines
at 45 degrees,

ukiyo-e rain,
corrugated tin

sheet rain over
the cherries. So

the rain proffers
shelter. From which

something sings
out of me; Donald

O'Connor winks,
watch it, kid, he

says, keep wavin'
your arms like that,

and a wet, sharp
thorn bush is going

to catch on to you.

LESSONS IN BEING ALONE

The wind begins:
offering oak leaves
ascent, whether
I look or not.

Next fire and cold
conspire for a
chaplinesque turn:
I learn vine stocks
catch on quickly,
and the long half-
life of coals under
astonishingly
white ashes.

The past does its part:
A borie, a round
tapering stone
hut, is empty, save
a small stone table.
I imagine
a shepherd stretch
a hide across
the opening.

By their rare
red: the wild hips.

Baguette and air:
It's hard to eat up
a loaf before
it dries. But magpies
swing by, there's trout
in the pond, and
bread gives body
to soup, or toasted
serves tapenade.

I: arrange my
daily treasure
on a white plate;
cuttings drying
in a shotgun
cartridge; three
kinds of tree snails,
two myrtle fruits,
one truffle.

Wind, my teacher,
returns: today
I am someone else,
mistral; I will
teach you to move
intently, you
don't need clouds.
Under blue skies,
I give you
clairvoyance.

COMING OUT OF ONE

In a spent shotgun cartridge,
a dry vase, I put lichen,
a branch full of seeds
sprouting cotton-like tails,
a sprig of russet leaves
whose gentle topside belies
the abiding prickliness
of what's underneath.

My first honorary degree
was from the Royal Institute
of Technology, Stockholm;
when they called up
the oldest of us
there was a loud boom –
I thought, now that's strange,
Nobel's country,
but they could have waited.
When the boom came
for the second of us, the man
next to me leaned over
and whispered –
a Navy boat is moored outside.
Such was the custom;
at dinner young girls
brought us "our" shell
full of summer flowers.

Twenty years pass;
I have not learned to hunt,
but pick up any shells
that come my way,
tree snails or gun.
I learned early to forget,
but I remember
(better now than then)
the shells in the bunkers
we played in in Germany.
You could smell the powder
in those shells.

In the new world
I made orbitals matter,
even come to peace
with quantum spookiness,
yet I still feel
like that two-faced leaf.

TWO TREES

Those who cull
left them side
by side close;
one trunk shades
a second.

Others cut
branches back,
left the dark
one two that
can't be shaded.

Desperate
for balance,
I think late
sun will switch
the trees' roles.

But parity
comes only
from the fire's
radiant light
in between.

TOHU VA'VOHU

I can't
cease
thinking
of the
form-
less
there,
before
a there
was
there;
the aether
of what
hazarded
to be.

Rabbi
Shlomo
Yitzhaki,
Rashi,
a vintner
in medieval
Troyes,
read
it so:
"astonishingly
empty,"
the world

before
God
put
his hand
to it.

Was it like
the Greenland
ice cap,
where
my daughter
stayed,
the
uneventful
horizon,
untouched
by mountain,
not to speak
of tree.
The purest
of white
circles,
when
you could see?

Here,
in Provence,
a bulldozed
mountain

of trunks,
roots, oh rings,
tangled
old vine.
The field
from where
this came
lies long,
plowed;
frost gathers
in the V's,
waiting,
for
new vines.

I'm with Rashi;
Yes,
the void
will be
filled,
either
by God's act
or mine (Rashi
wouldn't
have said that);
but
the over-
whelming
feeling is

awe,
that such
emptiness
could
simply
be!
Not
out,
there,
but
within.

BLACK ON BLACK

In Cracow, the old Jewish town
is manicured for tourists, with

Yiddish cafe signs, posters for
Schindler's List sights. There are few

tourists, but in an empty, white-
washed synagogue an endless tape

plays a black and white movie (German
footage) of the move into Kazimierz

ghetto in early '42:
poor people pushing wheelbarrows,

a well-dressed man in a horsedrawn
carriage, trunks piled high, a cart

carrying what looks to be a whole
hut, the driver, smiling, tipping

his hat to the German officers
(who are in the film, smiling too),

streaming crowds, crowds alive, children
watching an endless stream of

furniture crammed into a house. And I
think of the vineyard in Bonnieux:

on a newly carved out terrace,
along the stone wall the white shells

lie in clumps, some sunk into
the earth, some piled into small hills,

a mausoleum to themselves.
I imagine the snails alive,

moving to succor, moving, at
their own pace, to the last wetness

after a dry spell. Or so one could
try to explain, oh so one wants

to understand, those traces of life
still, or moving, white on white,
black on white.

II

POLAND 1941-4

THE GATE

One day I drove south of Beersheba
looking for desert, looking for a place

to cry for my father. I walked into a wadi
and when the road noise faded to a hum
I sat down to watch one survivor bush.

This was a place to remember, I thought,
a dry place, long out of tears. But an ant
crawled out near the root, then another.

Why can't we cry? Because we've cried
too long, inside. Because no tears are left;

to which a voice says: it's a renewable
resource, kid. No, when we were hiding
and a letter came that they killed him, she

did cry: he promised he'd come! She cried:
who knows where he lies. She cries:
I should have made him stay that time.

But there, then…she grew quiet, save
nights, when she thought me asleep, and

she wrote in the copybook he took notes
in German on relativity theory. Grownups
don't cry: no matter how old, a child

is a child – one must not cry in front of
a child. One must not take them to funerals.
It's like being locked outside of yourself.

And every crawl space to the man,
the man holding a child is nailed shut.

It's like a switch you flip, and it's off
every way. Permission comes, astonishing,
at night, it comes on a flickering screen

in its black and white dress: a small girl
with curls, on a perfect lawn, drinks tea.
She is told her collie is run over. And

you think, no! you feel, all the children
who were lost, who could not learn, who

would not drink hot cocoa with cream.
The mothers who would not cry. Boards
shatter, the way in, to yourself, gapes.

A child let me in; she cries, as I do.

TWO ROSES

bloomed in a Polish town.
In Hebrew they were
Shoshana; Suzanne
was a stretch for a Jew,
so one Roza, one Roiza.
Both – Reyzele. A brother
of one married a sister
of the other. Shoshanat
Yaakov, the rose of Jacob,
fragrant to their parents;
were there thorns, no one
now is left to remember.

The war came. One hot
summer Roza stood
with her parents for seven
days in our Złoczów square.
Waiting for a transport.
Her brother, my father,
passed, heard them begging
for water. The guards
raised their guns; he had a wife
and a child, he went on.
They stripped them for lice;
Roza stood naked, pink
in the eyes of her father.

In Polish gardens roses grew
well that last spring of the war.
Roiza and a friend lay hiding
in a barn, in mouldy blankets,
in their smell. For a while,
the Ukrainian who hid them
brought kielbasa, bread,
an old apple, water. He stopped,
they grew weak, and one day,
when he knew they couldn't
run, he brought the police.

All flowers wilt, all bushes die.
But not this way, not a cut rose.

THE GAZE

My mother says: "Every day
we looked death in the eye."

She's proud of her English.

"Were you scared, Mammi?"
"Yes," and then she smiles,
the rare smile of the sick:

"He looked away."

I was there. But a child
can't see. I imagine now

my mother, her brothers,

Aunt Nunia, I, in the attic,
in our long dark evenings,
for what if Dyuk's* neighbors

saw a light? There, death

comes riding, into small
village noises, Death,
with spats, holster,

a whip, breaking

branches as he rides, working
quietly his way through lists,
ridding green earth of a worm.

"In the eye": His roaming

stops, by Dyuk's school.
Inside, they hear hoofbeats,
that stop. Death spots them,

across two walls. And they
look him in the eye. But then
Death, boots, spurs and all,

smells stale cabbage soup,

which reminds him of the dead,
soiling themselves. He looks
away, fastidious death

And comes back
the next day.

*Dyuk was the family that hid us toward the end of the war.

THE EXCHANGE

"We have something we think is yours,
Pani Klara," said the daughter-in-law

of the man who hid us in an Univ attic
in forty three and four. Lyuba had come

to Brooklyn, to work for a year or two.
From her purse she took out a man's

gold ring, held it out to Mammi.
My mother, whose eyes had failed,

passed the ring to me. I made out
the engraved initials, F.R., and said,

"it's Uncle Fromcie's ring, I think,"
My uncle has a son. We paid them

in gold, at the end in jewelry, all we had.
But no gold could buy goodness, or life

not in those days, not in Ukraine.
I put the ring in my mother's palm.

In one motion, her wrinkled hand
steady as it had not been in years,

she gave it back to Lyuba. "It's yours."

RAT LANGUAGE

There's a woman trapped under a grate.
She spoke to me calmly, asking for help,
we must save her. But move slowly, for
she's grown in there, grown to the shape
of the sewer. Her bones must be bent
we can't just take her out. Her muscles
must be massaged. Before we walked out
in June forty four, walked from the Dyuks
to the Russian lines, did they massage
the men's legs, the stronger women?
They were swollen, there was no place
to walk in the storeroom where we hid,
the bunker we dug out under it.
We must lift her gently, with oil poured
round her, with a winch, there's time.
Please talk to her, ask her how she came
in the sewer, why her children left her,
was there a time she could lift the grate.
Ask her what food people threw her way;
where her patience came from. And who
else lived in the sewers, and did she
learn rat language. Meanwhile, I'll get help.

III
CRAFTS, PENLAND NC

CHOICE

Glass won't think. Red-
orange out of the furnace,
its mass wrapped
round a pipe, it cools
a dark red fades, revives
in the oven, sags a spell.
I would be glass, giving.

The glass-maker's control:
into the fire, he says, out.
He presses the glass
with cork boards, sparks
fly, his tongs constrain.
Glass plunged into water
and ashes, crackles, saved.
I would be the glass-maker.

But who controls whom?
Thought gone into feeling
in his hands, an arc
swung, and glass, only
glass could – stretches,
sets, one curve gently
nestled in another, near
as we were, to music.

Not too hot, not too cold;
even-tempered, annealed,
disorder flows, blessing
change in life's shape. Soon,
when we meet, will you
be glassmaker or glass?

BASKET PHILOSOPHY

for Billie Ruth Sudduth

to carry
somewhere
to someone
for a good
reason

to keep
something
meant
to be
kept
apart
safely kept
for someone

out of
something
grown
but cut
twisted
or shaved
so dead, yet

reborn,
no,
trans-
formed

in the hands
of someone
usually a woman

shared
space
carved
out of air
by one
over
the other
under

a construction
in which
you
can have
a stake
actually
you'd better
have many

a way of life
where
upsetting
is inevitable

where
the ends
need
to be
concealed
and the means
laid
bare.

stakes
high
stakes low
every basket
a gamble

along
a spoke
out of sight
 (but not of mind)
tapered
to be
hidden

not
the only
part of life
where
in and out
out and in

can
tire
some.

where
loose ends
are part
of the plan

and
entwinement
flirts
with
interpenetration

the lesson
of a basket
Billie Ruth's –
an elbow
can make
a heart.

THE ONE AND THE MANY

1

A wax nut I carved
turned (glory be
to polymers) into
three silicone
molds, to be
invested (more tech),
wax burned out,
metal streaming
through ample sprues.
Walnuts and pearls;
later we sold many.

2

You asked me
for a burr, to finish
the shell. And then,
oh it was June, we
walked into fireflies'
and stars' frame
for spruce and pine;
I stumbled, felt
your steady hand.

3

Bronze to silver,
one chain to many.
To break the mold
there came scallop
shells and nut meat.
I cast a strand
for you, one pearl
opened to a heart.

4

So we settled down
by the craft school,
as many. Carved
out life's wave in years
of diapers, Russian
kale, Sunday school.

5

In flux and fusion
heart beats the drum
walnuts leaf out,
we live on, in
in the fireflies' gold
and sundry glow.

STRONG FEELINGS
ABOUT DINNER PLATE DÉCOR

It's the curtain,
stage set, and
if you're hungry
the last thing
you see. A
chance to impress
before and after,
yes, an argument
for drama. But
food is the play.

A lot of what
makes me hungry
tends to brown,
like French toast
and onion rings.
Fryin' and bakin'
does it.
Not the same
being more fun
than the same
(see God's
first week), I'd
say – stay
away
from brown.

Except for some
kids I know,
most folks eat
from the outside
in, and don't
want to wait
too long to
be pleasured
by a pattern.
A lighter rim,
so you can spot
that red beet
contemplating
a dive onto
a white lace
tablecloth.

Food comes
as it gets to be:
organic, semi-
liquid, in slopes
and scallops
of collapsed
mashed potato
mounds, pea
landslides, gravy
congealed in
the memory of
being ladled

out, dressing
droplets shaped
by surface tension.
Looks good
against
a neat but un-
symmetrical grid.

I don't know
about you, but
my roast beef,
potatoes and
vegetable
of the day tends
to get messier
fork by fork.
A camouflage
net of beige
and green won't
make it easy
to sop up
the last bit.
Blue's a safe
bet for a pattern
and not just
in sky or jeans.
No food is blue.

Flowers, small
motifs, the calming
beat of repetition,
a gentle palette.
Food is rockin'
chair, mother
and grand-father,
home. The way
to your mouth
is not
in your face.

No worms
or snakes,
Francis Bacon
sides of beef.
For that matter –
no frolicking sheep,
or chickens.
Especially,
no calves
or suckling pigs.
Little fish are OK.

We're human, please
no concave
surfaces, no
knife traps in
corrugated terrain.

All this said
and done, it's not
that different from
marrying someone.
Oh, there's reason,
and parents will
tell you whom they
don't like. While you
just go on, and find
that special one
who is like your mother
or first wife.
Or not.
My mother used
to tell me – you sleep
where you make your
bed. And eat
from plates,
lovely plates,
made
to break
every rule.

TECTONICS

genesis

Not God, or Rabbi Loew.
Today it's just Roald,
squeezing a ball of clay,
his small stake in creation.
Did they begin this way,
two thumbs
hesitant in clay? Yes,
for now
there is the other,
a hole
in the wholly round.

he remembers

He was six;
June 1944, five Jews
walking out of hiding
to the Russian lines,
the fertile fields
sodden
in spring rains,
no way
but through the clay,
his uncles are leaning
on the women.
His mother carries him.

take clay

A thing with magic
begs
to be understood.
Kaolin and feldspar,
hydrated
aluminosilicates,
layer-like,
taking up water,
platelets sliding
past each other.
Reversible
to a point.
This lesson
May be of use,
but who
will do
the kneading?

centrifugal

in a world
of seductive
tugs out,
and not just
at the wheel,
all you can do

is keep plastic,
balance,
and build,
by hand,
the higher shape
within.

a hand

of clay is not
the clay hand
of a broken idol.
It's a woman
in Angola
reaching out
with a can of milk;
it's the hands,
now two,
moving nervously,
of a man
told his son
is missing
in Chechnya.

subtractive

so now
this wet object
faces me,
ample evidence
to being far out
of the creators'
league.
But God
was into salvage,
I recall, and
my teacher says
there are tools,
all those fingers,
a grater,
a curvy metal disk, and
this slip slurry.
Formation
is as much
a matter
of taking off
as adding on.

my hands

on the pot,
remember, oh,
how
they reached out
for yours,
hand
over hand,
one summer day.

where

people were, there
are shards.
There is clay
on my hands,
there is clay
in my hair.
It'll wash off.
Not the clay
in my heart.

WITH, OR AGAINST

From a worka-
day rusty bar

the saw cuts
a cube of steel.

Its face shines
bright, as love.

Welded in arc
and sparks

to a rod,
in and out

of a forge
spilling flame,

a steel cube
is swung to

anvil; it's
yellow-red,

like rose-hips
in our valley.

A woman,
bracing a

chisel, a man
swinging sledge-

hammer. Twenty
kinds of nerves

go to the hand.
Like the line cut

in the block, now
cooling, soon

to make patterns
in another, you

marked me. Do
we follow the

way of steel,
its impure

alloy strength?
A master smith

said: comply, but
contend – make

hard soft, hard
again, beat blade

and girder into
rabbit's ear and

morel. Love, oh
love for steel too,

is built sweet out
of strict desire,

for the you, that
is not you. You.

ALTERED

Tough beginnings,
but I'm not the
only one – torn
up, milled, sieved.
There were moments:
I felt hands round
me. And then fire.
Freezing me, till
you came, your lips.

Turn me, read in
my nakedness
marks of flame, salt,
air kept away,
the ghostly trace
of my support.
Look into me,
ring me. In your
gaze, I look back.

Nothing's perfect.
Rough, a patchwork
of repair cracks
in the telling
heat. Let others
dress me, stories
of design. I'm
what chance put in
your hand. You're mine.

DOES IT HURT TO KNOW?

1

The quiet wind's in this cloth,
blowing cross a repose
of indigo lines, in variant
space, there making them
touch, here not.

Fabric was wrapped snugly
spiraling up a tube, tied
in thread, pushed up
into bunched folds, dyed
and rinsed.

2

At the orb's edge, near
my light, in a curled leaf
waits this quarter-sized
yellow-marbled spider, all
carmine legs.

The capture silk stretches
up to three times, in runs
of five amino acids, dominant
glycine and alanine in long,
spring-like loops.

3

The ground is silk, shades
of bronze from a first bath,
now through it in red, poppy
red, meandering cracks stall
at an edge.

Here it's paste, good old
potato starch, cracking
like mud after rain, a resist
mid cloth and dye, chance
to order.

IV

DNA

In 2003, on the 50th anniversary of the Watson and Crick paper, Nature magazine asked me to write a poem for the occasion. In the end, they didn't like any of the three I did write…

MISIRLOU

By the full moon the hill
called, she climbed; her
time off the telescope.
Days, her eyes would go

to the canyons' green life,
but this night only pasture
lit up and the moon, well,
it just lorded over Hercules.

She thought: we're children
of a sun coalesced
from cinders, the debris
of dead stars, a fluke

of nuclear levels; this too
will burn out. And, pulling
her sweater around her,
she whispered to no one

in particular: I'm
alone on this hill, and
would lean against him,
his arms round me from

behind. This being sad, she
sang "Who's gonna shoe
my pretty little foot", which
made her feel a bit better,

and because it seemed fine
to keep on speaking, said
to the hill: those stones there,
must've been a slide; but

I suppose you don't need
to be told that, hill. And:
Why am I in this body,
when I see a billion years

in my star spectrum, ask
how retinal's made? And,
because she was alone
and sore troubled, the earth

answered her with slow signs.
The wind came first, swirled
her skirt. Then she heard
the swish surf of grass, and

listened, for the first time,
to its ancient stories
of shared genes of wheat,
hemp, and flax. The grass

liked her sweater, half linen,
half orlon. And the hill, well,
it spoke too, of hot springs,
silver vugs. She saw Orion,

near her signing galaxy.
No longer alone, the tune,
of all things, in and out,
could be summoned — for this

the moon gave her leave. She
took it, stretched her arms, and
on the cowpaths taught all
her dance, the Misirlou.

SUSTAINABLE DEVELOPMENT

Alive? The
vines just push
the question

aside, a
green muff for
these trees, coat-

ing them real
tight like a
crosslinked po-

lymer gone
mad. The prob-
lem in spring

is the trees' —
are they? And
will they be?

Or, will vine
stop in sym-
biotic

rhyme, leaving
leaves an a-
nodyne space,

another
shade, to soak
dear photons

from the sun?
Or will it
take no less

than the mo-
lecular
mojo, the

shapeliest
wrench insid-
iously bound

in a groove
in the vine's
codehoarding

antipa-
ralel inner
twine. Upscale

we, no time
for evo-
lution, grip

culture's hand-
me-downs – clo-
thing and moods –

for one I
would this vine
grow to sub-

stitute bark.
The twining
attachment

that may throt-
tle starts in-
nocently,

yes, in spring,
like the first
gentle leaning

of the cree-
per on the
tree. We think

we have choice,
to cut, in
time. But this,

like a dark
green beeswarm,
grows, divine.

CODE, MEMORY

Alcman, they say, called her big-eyed,
since we see the past by our thinking

Walk in, to a Ticino alp's
wild strawberry midsummer,
see the blues flit, conjure up

a young Russian with a net.
Elsewhere, by lamplight,
one you loved can look

at the old photos and say
"you smile like your father,
he also wore a cap."

The way lit up in '53,
two young men just willing
a model into being. Walk,

toward them, past a monk
tending peas, on to stains,
agar plates and centrifuges,

come, walk by the light
of signals from within, past
x-shaped diffraction patterns;

on, past '53, heady
with the logic of splice
and heal, the profligate

wonder of polymerases,
into denominable bounty,
down this biochemical

rope trick of a molecule,
its rings' sticky signposts
tied to a backbone (chain,

chain, chain, she sings)
run – of sugars, unsweet,
and phosphate triads.

There, there's memory's lair,
the inexpungable trail
of every enzyme that worked,

and those that did but
for a while, every affair
the senses had with a niche,

the genes turned off
as we came out of water,
what worked, what nearly killed –

the insinuating virus, code
immured in coiled softness,
coopted symbiotes. Move,

for here wiggling and collision
gauge shape, down necklaces
of meaning interrupted

by stutters, the ons, offs,
intent, a tinkerer's means
to function (that escapes us),

on, to difference, earthy life,
its dendral arms hazarding
berry and you, to the butterfly

that lights on torn up earth
in Srebrenica and Złoczów,
that flies to the far place

love obstinately chose.
An Alp… is to be climbed;
they did, our mid-century

helixeers. But oh, an alp
is also a sweet shoulder
of a mountain, that meadow

reaching for snowline, the place
where men drive cattle, rest,
move higher. An alp is clover,

a place to feed, and watch
another blue, now the morning
glory's winding grasp and

climb. The word sings, in alp
and alkaline phosphatase
and DNA, in nuanced refrain;

this side of memory, of a world
that was; and one that will be.

V

HITOKOTO-NUSHI

They tell stories of the Buddhist ascetic En-no-gyōja, who grew strong, so that he could compel a native mountain god to do his bidding. So Hitokoto-nushi, god of Katsuragi, Lord of one word, grumbling but obedient, built the great bridge between Katsuragi and Yoshino. But they say the mountain god moved stones only in the dark of night, lest he scare his people.

THE GOD'S FACE

1

On the way to Yoshino's
sakura blossoms, late
one night, I saw a row
of shops lining the way
to the god's bright red shrine.

2

The first stall made yuba, skimming
the skin off boiling soy milk, folding
it into sticks. I bought a sheet
wrapped round a pickle, and pulled
out of my rucksack a bean pod,
wound it up. It scuttled sideways,
twisting like a caterpillar. "Clever,"
the man said, "did you make it?" "I did.
It's yours." He shook my hand, beaming.

3

I went up the hill, though I heard
behind me the yuba maker say
"A bean fell out." On, to a stand
of sashes, kimonos, bags. I bought
a jinbei, and gave the woman
a metal cicada that leaped and
every time it landed changed color.
She clapped her hands, "It's just right
for my cloth shop! How good you are!"

4

She wound it up, the insect sprung,
I heard her giggle and then cry
"oh, oh," but I was already
looking at sorobans up the hill –
their heavenly beads, their earth beads
carved and lacquered, black and red,
their rods bamboo. I took out my
best, a hula girl juggling black
and white hourglasses. "It's for you,"
Putting his glasses on, the man said
"Such work has not come this way."
"I made it; it's the way I count.
But she's a bit naughty behind."

5

I gave away the troll with sparks,
the filigree-winged butterfly, and
the bus whose tires deflated, revived.
All I had. But things fell apart;
the shopkeepers ran up, cried: "Your
monkey stopped flipping." "A gear broke."
"The wheel came off." I tried to fix them,
right there, but parts were missing, tools
not at hand, and I had lost my skill.

6

I ran to the shrine, to hide,
to sleep. In the morning
there stood the god, hiding
his ugly face behind a fan.
He said: "And what wind-up
toy is there for me?"
"I have no more," I shook
my pack. "You've made my folk
unhappy." "I gave them…
gifts. I bought their wares."
"What will you give me?" he said.
"All I have left. My face,
my love." And I took hold
of his rough bridge-builder's
hand, and led him, to dawn.

A WEED, A GOD

More than ever I want to see
in these blossoms at dawn
the god's face.
　　　　Matsuo Bashō

Here, the weed the jeep crushed will rise up;
it has lived through worse, that scraggly plant,
a seasoned refugee from agro schemes
for prepped fields, genes crafted into berries
to thwart pesticides that wilt past snap-back.
A survivor, the weed emigrates to gullies.

Crossing the god's bridge, people now drive
to misty Yoshino to watch the sakura cherry
(*Prunus serrulata*) bloom. The pink blossoms
signal transience in their free-floating
yet certain fall; we see the steady march
of the spring cherry season up Japan.

The weed and I, cousins at some remove,
did race down a hall of chemical mirrors.
In us confined congeries of enzymes
brew life, and coopting chance, find
forked ways to breathe, range, and re-
construct. These I would know, for pretty
or ugly, we wouldn't be if the weed weren't.

In the sakura blossoms the sensitive god's face
hides in pink shimmers. I look for him here too,
in the shadows that flit behind the petals,
What moved him will never be simple, and
the veil we'll lift may show a face terrible
with viruses passed on god to us, trapped
in our genes, in molecules as benign
as venomous. And maybe kindnesses
will come too, in the tinkerer's edgy
patch on the gentle echo of the weed.

THE MOUNTAIN GOD

As the story begins, a Buddhist ascetic
in the forest drinks only from the dew
on pine needles, stands under cold falls

night after night, with his ax and his conch.
In time, En could fly on a cloud of five colors,
and bind spirits, even his own mountain's

Hitokoto-nushi, Lord of one word,
he who takes on questions in one word, gives
counsel in one, too. The story tries to move on

as stories do – I stay with the mountain god.
In his shrine I'd ask why my father died,
But in one word? I try: "Father,"

Hitokoto-nushi understands, gods do,
he answers, "You." Done
thinking, I am set free, cry. In time

the story reasserts itself, it tells how
En-no-gyōja ordered the god to build
a bridge from Katsuragi to Yoshino;

of stone and wood the god built it. They say
Hitokoto-nushi worked only nights
so that people not see his hideous face.

This god will not let me go; now his care
puzzles me. For they are old, the guardians
of torrents, clouds, the banyan and redwood gods.

What are we to them – the earth was before us,
and will remain. Though we cut trees, and level
mountains - oh, where will you flee, dear old ones?

Gods need be terrible; for Hitokoto-nushi
I think up a monstrous guardian demon face,
curled red flesh, indigo nails. But that he care?

I imagine a child was kind to him,
and then ran off, frightened by his face. I
imagine the god loved a girl in Nara,

and in love's quiet afterglow slipped back
into his spirit form. I imagine
a traveler come to see the cherries,

shared a yuba-wrapped pickle with the god.
The mountain god was sad, his people fled
from him. If I were to meet the god, alone

on a moonless night, I would summon up
my father's desperate courage. Or try.
And with the memory of close love, reach

past loss, past pink blossom veils. I'd ask
the god teach me, in his one word: forgive.

VI

SCIENCE

KAMCHATKA

From Vietnam era helicopters
you first see "smoke". Closer,
the lakes and broken rim
of Uzon caldera paint in steam
a Monet land, blues and yellows,
Up close, pool upon pool, crystal
clear, one on the way to orange,
bubbles plopping threateningly
through the mud clay of another.

And life, in every shade but green.
For this isn't the photosynthetic
world – my silver rings turn black
from hydrogen sulfide. Water
bubbles up boiling at 95°C; pH
paper makes out that water acid
as nitric, elsewhere drain-cleaner
basic; I'd not touch it cool. Round
each pool, life – dull red, yellow,
beige mats of bacteria, archaea.

Eight months of the year, Uzon
caldera is under snow. Water,
seeping down to the magma
is shot up, in percolating flow
depositing, dissolving. This is
geochemistry in the fast forward
mode – here realgar, pyrite,
five meters down maybe gold.

Some like it hot. Some want O_2,
some do not. This niche came,
the rest – evolution's game
tinker; give it time, hazard, and.
from C, N, H, O, S, metals, life
finds its way; those mats – in
a hell of acid and heat (to us) –
find a dear place to play, and
pry survival out a few genes.
Pyrolobus fumarii grows best
at one hundred and thirteen °C.

It's not done with mirrors, but
in watery molecular strategems.
Eggs (protein too), would cook,
cell walls melt in Uzon's pools.
Hyperthermophiles, the same
and not the same, in their walls
an ether linkage brace, proteins
made tough by straight runs of
resistant amino acids, and DNA,
finds bodyguards in polyamines,
basic proteins, reverse gyrases,
and a really good repair shop.

So they adapt, like the folk
who live here, who serviced
the submarines of the old
USSR, and now that the ships

rust and midwinter electricity
is on but three hours a day,
they are still here, sell berries
and black radishes at market,
drive stolen Japanese cars,
eat fish at every meal, drink.
They are here, at the periphery,
nine hours flight from Moscow,
where eagles feed their young,
the earth trembles, bears pace
the streams when salmon run.

And some of us are fishers
of archaea, if not of men
or salmon; will you eat sulfur,
or hydrogen, or iron salts; we,
so smart, would know how –
there's acid, heat, dazzle us
oh organism with your holistic
web of tricks! And some of us
are newfangled fishers –
for DNA, for isn't it all, all
that matters? That makes you
puffer fish or mouse, inscribes
in a four letter code blueprints
for every inner assembly line?
Who knows, the hot spring's dirt
might hide a billion dollar gene.
And what will Kamchatka get?

On a piece of walrus scrimshaw,
a well-dressed Russian bear
rests on a sled. He's tired, like
our students after a long day's
collecting, who now sit cross-
legged on the floor, stabilizing
their DNA. The bear holds
in his hands a steaming cup,
there's a kettle on the snow.
Somewhere there must be a fire;
behind him a smoking volcano.
Kamchatka, bearing sweet life.

SCIENCE

for E. A. Socolow

Some say
it's a clue to the source, or
warrants for heaven on earth deluxe.
Some say
it's just caging nice birds,
blinders, or worse.
But I tell you,
it's giving things
their voice.
At first they're mute,
only their needs
manifest, like a baby's,
the mad green foliage craving light,
the red blood
starved for oxygen.
Their first words
are coaxed out
by the spectrometer's light:
magnesium...iron. In time
we learn to have a conversation, they and I.
They tell me: around the metal
mother, the tinkerer,
has forged this organic band
(and here we forget the world,
children in our secret language),
uroporphyrinogen-III,
this wheel of life,

four ganged rings, each given
a sense, three one way,
the fourth reversed. They draw you out,
in the lab we talk all night
of roots and reasons. And
they're choosy, these rings,
these colored things;
to an Englishman, not me,
they bare a family secret —
that last, weird ring
is put in right, then
flipped, in vivo.
What will they say next,
and to whom,
these inconstant gossipers,
these loud-mouth things?

THE STRUGGLE OF FACTS WITH LIFE

for Ciel Bergman

The nested gilt boxes
in Tomb KV-62
wait for Howard Carter
till 1925 when
he opens the next to last
mummy case and 110
kilograms of gold shine
as the day they were sealed
in Tutankhamen's tomb

I love 22-carat facts

It's dense, a quart of it
weighs 40 pounds.
Heavy metal tungsten
beats it by a hair, osmium
iridium, platinum
and rhenium by a lot.

Unconcerned with density,
a Moche smith beats
on the copper-gold alloy;
denser gold migrates
to the surface; he smiles
at his gleaming secret.

My granddaughter smiles.

80% of elements
are metals, their silvery sheen
a property of their common
free electrons. The metallic
reflection spectrum of gold
(and copper) is different.

Are there red metals, or green?

Yes, but they're not elements,

Gold is rare, but not too rare
Found everywhere, so
made for commerce. And
in native form. not waiting
for someone to win it
from an ore. Gold's ions crave
electrons; strip them even
from water, to form the metal.
While iron rusts, dissolves.

You can't make a good sword
out of gold.

You can buy the best one
for gold.

Malleable, and ductile…

-able and –ile. Poor metal,
to have all this done to you.

A way in to the goldsmith

in the service of vanity

and art. Listen – gold
can be beaten with mallets
into fine foil sheets,
one ten-thousandth
of a millimeter thin; one
ounce makes 20 square meters

Facts kill a poem

Fat cats kill a poem

Aureus, 20-stater, florin, ducat
doubloon, vreneli, sovereign,
gold eagle, krugerrand, koban,
solidus, dinar, moidore

People will kill for gold

People will cut your head off,
and sever your limbs,
cut your torso in two, even
3230

years after you die.
Avoid Howard Carters.

In Goldwasser from Danzig
now Gdansk, in Indian pastry.
Aloof, harmless as a metal.
Solutions of its ions poison,
yet a new drug for arthritis.

Cyanide to extract it,
from low-grade ores, yet
fewer killed by that lethal
chemistry than by mercury,
in the Pantanal, where
miners make amalgams;
the mercury burned off
in the assayers' shops
into their lungs.

Across the mountains, Andean
metalsmiths trusted the mix
of alum, saltpeter and salt
to dissolve gold. They dip
a copper mask in the slurry.
A thin gold film, looking for
all the world as electroplated
waits to be annealed.

A mouthful of gold
in that Uzbek smile.
while in America, it hides
under porcelain.
And in the camps
the kapos pulled teeth
of corpses and prodded
women's privates for
gold coins, to fill trains
sent to Swiss banks

You never trust it's pure:
The assayer's bone ash
cupel, in it the ore, added
lead – melt, slag oxides
float, gold sinks.

You never trust anyone
around it, many things
look like gold - pyrites
brass, titanium nitride

At times we want things
to look like other things

When I see the photos
of Tutankhamen's tomb
I don't look at the gold, I see
the chariot, chairs, boats

all neatly stacked for
a journey to the afterworld.

Or the nanoworld; where tiny
gold crystals form on adding
citrate to ion solutions:
colloidal gold, like milk, but
in transparent deep red
to violet liquids. Ruby gold,
the jewel of stained glass.

The painter who sees gold
in her future, brought gold paint
and markers, gold leaf. And violet
pigments. She has a chance

of letting the gold facts live.

VII
SANTA CRUZ MOUNTAINS

CLOSE ENCOUNTERS
OF THE FOURTH KIND

A brain is lying on the ranch road.
"Dr. X," it says, in a quiet southern
voice. I look around to see if anyone
else is there, but it sure looks like

the same dirt road I've hiked before.
So I squat down, to hear it better,
and, I have to confess, to see if it's
growing out of the ground, "Dr. X?"

it asks, "I'm not Dr. X, brain."
"Oh, I'm so happy you aren't." This
is getting more complicated by the
minute, but, hey, it's California.

I take a stab, "Are you from his lab?"
"No... well, yes. Frankly... I escaped,"
the brain says, real matter-of-fact.
Can't think of any Dr. X, though

who knows what Stanford's artificial
intelligence lab is up to. I sneak
a look at those hemispheres; didn't
recall they're split so much. "Brain,

you don't seem to have your life-support
along." I worry – the wind is picking up
and the brain, well, it's moist-looking,
as I imagine brains ought to be. And

sitting there among the chamomiles,
not quite your sterile environment.
"Yes, I had to leave in a hurry." This
sounds like one cool brain. "I can't

see you, there was no time to take
the eyes I'm hooked up to." I try
to visualize Dr. X's lab, but what I say
is "I've never met a talking brain."

"You mean yours doesn't talk to you?"
Wow. "Well, mine's… a bit of a mess."
"But you've met people who talk
as if they didn't have a brain?"

I whistle, while trying to figure this out.
This brain has … attitude. "Listen, brain,"
I say, "We've got to get you out
of the road, some folks might just

drive over you. No brain…er. Ha ha.
The brain doesn't laugh. "Well, Dr. …"
"Roald. But you can call me Pooh."
"Roald, just pick me up with your

surgical gloves." "Brain, this is a ranch,
we ain't got no surgical gloves."
Well, I wasn't going to pick the brain up
with my hands. So I rip two pages out

of the notebook I carry, for moments
of inspiration, you know, and slip it, or try,
under the brain. "Easy does it," he says.
Back at the ranch the brain is a big hit

with the artists; the talk drifts around
to left side, right side stuff. On which
the brain, after a drink, opines "As Hank
says, my left side knows my right sides'

cheatin' heart." "You're mixing metaphors,
brain!" "Roald, you are a bear of little…
and I am the source of all metaphor."
I try to get back at the brain, quoting

what I just learned about the neocortex
not being where emotions rise. Just then
the power goes kaput. The next day,
my brain is gone, leaving on the counter
a CD of Johny Cash's greatest hits.

JUST WHEN WE ARE SAFEST

In this approximant to paradise
there are no forbidden trees

and after you grow accustomed
to the wonder of fairy rings

a hundred feet tall, and trails
softer than any carpet, to moss,

the small cones and ferns,
you walk, at peace, to the meter

of your breath. Until, following
a stone up a road cut, the shrub:

the beat, it stops, the wind
in the redwoods is not there.

Part stiff, vibrating in resist; part
supple, like a willow. A branch

going straight, then jigs a wild
angle turn that cuts sharp the air,

leaving (no leaves) a hard notion
of what curve might be. No bark

just what seems skin, charged
yet smooth – ochre to orange,

green rising, its sleek reaching
for your hand; there are scales

that brush off; you want to do it,
to see if the gloss can bear

a mark. And then, near sherry
smooth bark-skin goes matte

all light is sopped up, and
dry ranges of warm browns

darken to a threatening purplish
tinge, like the stone-beat

indigo fabrics of west Africa,
like the bronze of metal-

ammonia solutions – I touch it.
The manzanita is philosophy,

of virtue – of branching, and
the matte purple bark sublime.

UNDER THE LINTEL

on Soda Gulch Trail, for Wolfgang Mastnak

In the middle there was a place for me
to stand, touch red-brown bark on each

fairy-ring tree. Then the eyes take charge,
soar up the bare trunks to the overlapping

small branches the loggers burned. A sukka
of redwoods, but its roof is full of life,

the texture of Egyptian palm fronds.
Up there I am set adrift by branches

that may go down, but the eye pulls up
to a dome, I try to undo the logic

of a strange vertical vanishing point.
So a glance up this second growth

of hundred-year old stolid cylinders
ends up in gaudy uncertainty, there

where the late afternoon sun, up to its
metamorphoses, crafts green and gold

organic stained glass in the leading
of branches an arm thick. In this narrow

cathedral I could write crazed sermons,
fly past desire, rest. Here you can't hood

your eyes; here, you are drawn, you
and not you, under the lintel, rising, up

to it, out of your self, alone, above.

SECOND GROWTH

Everywhere, redwood stumps

El Corte de Madera; but not all trees
served – the live oak and madrone
they let be, and when ground shook
and San Francisco had to be rebuilt,
they cut the sequoia, they cut clear
the tree called sempervirens.

100-year old stumps, still solid

Tough wood. Five feet above-
ground the fellers cut notches
for springboards where they stood
with 12 foot saws. Teams of oxen,
later steam donkeys, their winches
straining waited to pull the logs
on skids uphill. In the air – cursing
cracking whips and kerosene.

Moss on every brown stump

and live oak, lichen on every rock
and the concrete sculpture; ferns,
creambush and gooseberries
grow in the shadows. A squirrel leaves
neat sections of an acorn on the stump.

A fairy ring, second growth

not of mushrooms up through needles,
but now of hundred-year-old trees.
What clones – poking holes in the sky,
gently hugging the stump. On the ground,
the surprising small cones of redwoods
echo the reddish brown of bark and burl,
each cone a cathedral of spiky futures.

A road is cut out of paradise

Where this one-time logging road
was widened, clay and loose stone
wash down in spring; last year
a redwood, its roots weakened,
fell across. Where they cut it, I count
150 rings. This road asks for care
in its own second growth.

The road you and I will travel

is one that has been touched
by Pacific mist, by people.
The cultivated land, the stump,
cattle crossing, the hip rose.
Tenants in common – redwood
and coyote, a poet – cross
paths, flinch, and feed, tenants
in perpetuity on a blue world.

With Adam I and Adam II

The beginning was doubled:
bright stark ingenuities given
to the first Adam and Eve;
tomorrow their brood will find
microbes to feed on plastic
bottles and caps floating in
the North Pacific Gyre, and,
elsewhere, turn them to roads.
Past dominion, they will walk
hand in hand with the children
of those who till and tend, of
the second Adam, needing Eve.
Together, they build this road.

A road out of paradise, for you and me

does not stretch ahead on land alone,
it flies with the hawk, and plunges into
every phosphorescent bay, and down
the dark, deep underwater canyons.
We will walk that road, you and I, dance
down it in life's samba, like scuttling crabs
– people, dear people… and manzanita
and machines – aware of the one earth,
comingling strategies and wisdoms,
in slow fixes, earth healing at our touch.

ABOUT THE AUTHOR

ROALD HOFFMANN was born in 1937 in Złoczów, then Poland, now Ukraine. After surviving the Nazi occupation and after several years of postwar wandering in Europe, he and his mother and stepfather made their way to the United States in 1949, settling in New York City. He graduated from P.S. 16, Brooklyn, Stuyvesant High School, Columbia University, and from Harvard University with a Ph.D. in chemical physics. Since 1965, Hoffmann has been engaged in teaching and research in theoretical chemistry at Cornell University, where he is now Frank H.T. Rhodes Professor of Humane Letters Emeritus. In chemistry he has taught his colleagues how to think about electrons influencing structure and reactivity, and won most of the honors of his profession.

Hoffmann is also a writer – of poetry, essays, non-fiction, and plays – carving out his own land between poetry, philosophy, and science.

Hoffmann had his first real introduction to poetry at Columbia from Mark Van Doren, the great teacher and critic whose influence was at its height in the 1950's. He began to write poetry in the mid-seventies, but it is only in 1984 that his work began to be published. Hoffmann owes much to a poetry group at Cornell that included A. R. Ammons, Phyllis Janowitz and David Burak, as well as to Maxine Kumin. His poems have appeared in many magazines and several anthologies, have been translated into French, German, Portuguese, Russian, Spanish, Catalan (10 poems), Galician (6 poems), Polish, Croatian and Swedish. Six collections of his poetry have been published previously, including bilingual collections in Spanish in Madrid, and in Russian in Moscow. Hoffmann also writes nonfiction (five books) and plays (three plays produced).

Other books by Roald Hoffmann
published by Dos Madres Press

Something That Belongs To You (2015)

For the full Dos Madres Press catalog:
www.dosmadres.com